EXTREME HABITATS

DESERTS

Jim Pipe

Consultant: Greg Aplet Ph.D., The Wilderness Society

ticktock

Copyright © ticktock Entertainment Ltd 2007
First published in Great Britain in 2007 by ticktock Media Ltd.,
Unit 2, Orchard Business Centre, North Farm Road,
Tunbridge Wells, Kent, TN2 3XF

ticktock project editor: Rebecca Clunes
ticktock project designer: Sara Greasley, Hayley Terry

ISBN 978 1 84696 500 5
Printed in China
A CIP catalogue record for this book is available from the British Library.

Picture credits
t=top, b=bottom, l=left, r=right, f=far
Alamy Tim Hurst/Alamy 20t, Suzy Bennett/Alamy 26c, Robert Harding Picture Library Ltd/Alamy 27fb;
Corbis Hubert Stadler/Corbis 11b, Peter Lillie/Gallo Images/Corbis 14r, Hugh Sitton/zefa/Corbis 27ft; Robert Cameron/**Getty** 29t;
NASA 10t; Charles M. Omnanney/**Rex Features** 12-13; **Shutterstock** 2, 4-5 (all), 6-7, 7t, 7c, 7b, 8-9b, 10-11, 10b, 11t, 12l,
12r, 13l, 13r, 14-15, 16-17 (all), 18-19 (all), 20b, 21 (all), 22t, 22b, 23cb, 25ft, 25cb, 25fb, 26b, 27ct, 27cb, 28t, 28b, 29c;
Ticktock Media Archive 1, 3, 6t, 8t, 8-9t, 9t, 9b, 14l, 15,23ft, 23ct, 23fb, 24t, 25ct, 26t, 29b, 32
All artwork Ticktock Media Archive
Every effort has been made to trace the copyright holders, and we apologise in advance for any unintentional omissions.
We would be pleased to insert the appropriate acknowledgments in any subsequent edition of this publication.

CONTENTS

DRY, HOT AND EMPTY?

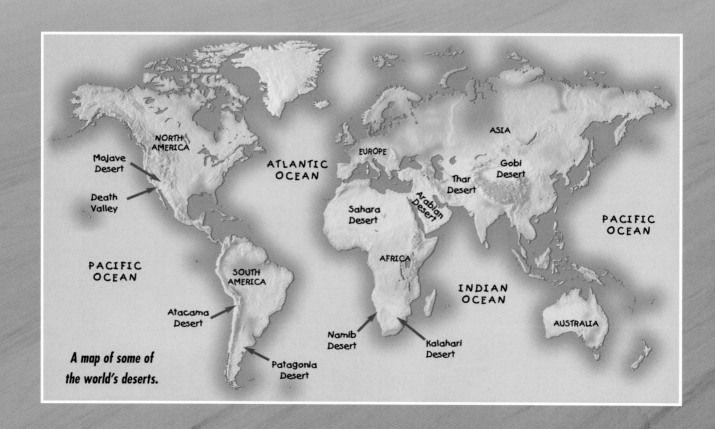

The red-barred dragon is a lizard found in some Australian deserts.

The ground under your feet is sandy and dry. There are no clouds in the sky and the Sun is burning hot. Not a sound can be heard and nothing moves. The desert all around you is lifeless... or is it?

Look closer, and you will find small **mammals** and lizards hidden in shady nooks. Under the ground, millions of plant seeds wait for the rains to fall.

NORTH AMERICA

Mojave Desert

Death Valley

ATLANTIC OCEAN

EUROPE

ASIA

Gobi Desert

Thar Desert

Arabian Desert

Sahara Desert

PACIFIC OCEAN

PACIFIC OCEAN

SOUTH AMERICA

AFRICA

INDIAN OCEAN

Atacama Desert

Namib Desert

Kalahari Desert

AUSTRALIA

Patagonia Desert

A map of some of the world's deserts.

In fact, thousands of animals and people live in deserts. Despite the heat, the lack of water and the blinding **sandstorms**, they survive. Could you?

A desert is a place where very little rain falls. Many deserts are also scorching hot, but not all. Some deserts can get very cold, such as the **Gobi Desert** in Asia.

DESERT NOTEBOOK

- A desert is a place that gets less than 25 centimetres of rain or snow each year.

- Even if a desert is very hot in the day, it gets extremely cold at night.

- Sand covers only about 20 per cent of Earth's deserts.

Fennec fox

- From space, deserts look empty and lifeless. But lots of different animals live in deserts. Many of them only come out at night, like the fennec fox.

DESERT SURVIVAL TIPS

Even if you don't feel thirsty, drink up! In a hot desert, an adult needs to drink 10-15 litres of water every day.

JOURNEY INTO THE DESERT

White clothing reflects the sunlight and keeps the wearer cool.

Deserts are beautiful but deadly. In a hot desert, a healthy person left without water and shade in the morning could be dead by the evening.

Out of the shade, the hot Sun quickly burns your skin. The heat makes you sweat, so your body loses lots of water even when you are sitting in the shade.

If you are planning a trip into the desert, make sure you bring the right gear! The desert Sun is very harsh and will quickly burn bare skin. Sunblock, light clothes and wide-brimmed hats will keep the Sun off your body. At night it can get very cold, so you will also need thick jackets and sleeping bags.

Travel is difficult. Cars and trucks can get bogged down in the soft sand.

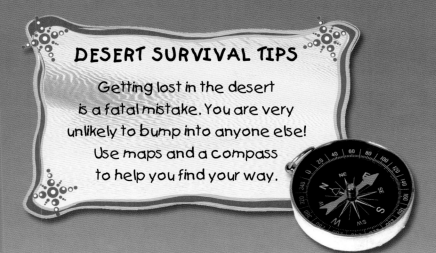

DESERT SURVIVAL TIPS

Getting lost in the desert is a fatal mistake. You are very unlikely to bump into anyone else! Use maps and a compass to help you find your way.

Bring water – lots of it! Many expeditions carry big water containers on trucks. If you do manage to find water, a **water filter** will make it safe to drink.

Be prepared for extreme weather such as sandstorms. Lightning can also be frequent in deserts, even if there is no rain.

DESERT NOTEBOOK

• Very few desert animals can kill a person, but spiders, scorpions and snakes can give you a nasty bite or sting.

The poisonous horned adder lives in the Kalahari Desert.

• More people drown in the **Sahara Desert** than die from thirst. That's because when it rains, dry **valleys** can turn into surging rivers in a few minutes.

Lightning strikes are so hot they can turn sand into glass. The sand forms a tube shape called a fulgurite.

THE LARGEST DESERT

The Sahara is by far the biggest hot desert in the world. It is about the same size as the United States. It stretches over 5,000 km from the Atlantic Ocean to the Red Sea. If you get lost in a desert this size, no-one will hear you scream!

If you walked across the Sahara Desert, you would find many different landscapes. You would cross **sand dunes**, gravel plains and rocky uplands. In the middle of the desert, you'd climb tall mountains with snowy peaks.

Camels are used to transport passengers and cargo in the Sahara Desert.

The huge sand dunes of the Sahara are known as **ergs**. Sand dunes form where something, such as a plant, blocks the wind and sand builds up against it.

Ergs in the Sahara often form crescent shapes.

Desert peoples survive by wandering from one **oasis** to the next. An oasis is a green spot in a desert where plants can grow all year. The Sahara has 90 large oases where people live in villages and grow crops. But you can't always rely on an oasis – sometimes the water runs dry.

DESERT NOTEBOOK

- 8,000 years ago the Sahara was covered in grasslands and forests. Cave paintings from this time show giraffes, elephants, and crocodiles.

Cave paintings in the Sahara

- The Sahara is bigger than the next eight biggest deserts put together.

- The world's highest sand dunes are in the north-east part of the Sahara. They are 465 metres tall, about the same as the Petronas Twin Towers, the world's second highest building.

DESERT SURVIVAL TIPS

Some Saharan scorpions can kill a human with one sting from their tail. In the desert never put your hands or feet where your eyes can't see!

THE ULTIMATE DUST BOWL

The **NASA** robot Zoë collects data
from the Atacama Desert.

The Atacama Desert stretches along the coast of Chile, between the Pacific Ocean and the Andes Mountains. It is the driest desert in the world. In the very driest parts, scientists have found no signs of life. Even bacteria can't survive here.

The **Atacama Desert** is a **rain shadow desert**. A rain shadow desert forms when tall mountains block rain clouds from reaching the other side. The Andes Mountains block clouds blowing in from the east, and they release their rain before they can reach the Atacama Desert.

Only a few tough plants can survive in the Atacama Desert. They collect moisture from the **sea-fog** that rolls in from the Pacific Ocean. In many years, fog is the only water the desert gets.

This sandy, rocky landscape is typical of the Atacama Desert.

DESERT SURVIVAL TIPS
Heatstroke can cause vomiting, confusion and blackouts. Drink lots of water and seek shelter. Use the shade of your car if you have nothing else.

Deserts are dry because the ground loses water faster than rain can keep the ground moist. Water drains away, or dries up and goes into the air as **water vapour**.

Space scientists visit the Atacama Desert to help them discover how they might look for life on the dry landscape of Mars.

DESERT NOTEBOOK

- In parts of the Atacama Desert, no rainfall has ever been recorded.

A flock of flamingos

- Flocks of flamingos live around the Atacama salt lakes. They feed on red **algae** that grow in the waters. This gives them their pink colour.

This modern concrete statue is 11 metres tall. It stands in the heart of the Atacama Desert, and many tourists go to see it every year.

The Equator

The Equator is an imaginary line around the centre of the Earth.

HOT AS AN OVEN?

Many of the world's deserts are found about 3,000 km north and south of the Equator. Here there are few clouds to shield the ground. The deserts are roasting hot in the day, and freezing cold at night.

Many deserts are not hot all year round. Their temperatures change with the seasons. A gentle hike through the Mojave Desert, in the USA, in January could turn into a fight for survival in July.

Some of the hottest temperatures ever recorded were in **Death Valley** in the Mojave Desert in 1917. For 43 days in a row, the maximum temperature was over 48°C.

The smooth, flat surface of Black Rock Desert in Nevada, USA is perfect for land speed record attempts. In 1997, the Thrust SSC reached a record-breaking speed of 1,227.9 kilometres per hour.

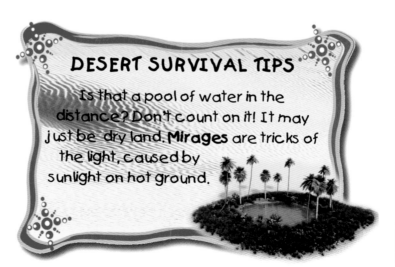

DESERT SURVIVAL TIPS

Is that a pool of water in the distance? Don't count on it! It may just be dry land. **Mirages** are tricks of the light, caused by sunlight on hot ground.

Lakes that have dried up leave behind a large area of flat land. They are ideal for breaking world speed records.

The flat, empty desert allowed Thrust SSC to become the first car to break the sound barrier.

DESERT NOTEBOOK

- The highest temperature ever recorded was at Al'Aziziyah in Libya in Africa. In September 1922 the thermometer reached a blistering 57.8°C.

Some deserts are so hot that you could fry eggs on the rocks.

- The world's longest hot spell was at Marble Bar in Australia, where the temperature reached 38°C or higher for 160 days in a row.

- The change from blazing heat during the day to freezing cold at night is enough to make rocks crack. Some split at night with a loud bang.

DESERT STORMS

Sandstorms can leave a thick coating of dust and sand on plants, animals and houses.

Grains of sand as seen under a microscope.

Do you think deserts are still and peaceful? Think again. Deserts are among the windiest places on Earth. The blazing Sun bakes the ground and heats the air above it. The hot air rises, and cooler air rushes in to take its place. This creates wind – lots of it.

Fierce desert winds create amazing sculptures from rock. The sand wears away softer rock faster, leaving the harder rock standing.

The speed and direction of the winds change constantly. This creates arches and giant stacks of rock, as well as strange-looking pillars and mushroom shapes called **hoodoos**.

DESERT NOTEBOOK

- Strong winds blow all year long in some parts of the Gobi Desert, pushing the sand along. Even the biggest sand dunes move about 50 metres a year.

Two kite buggies race across the desert.

- In 2006, 300,000 tonnes of sand were whipped up by a single sandstorm in the Gobi Desert. The storm dumped this sand on the city of Beijing, over 1,600 km away!

DESERT SURVIVAL TIPS

If you get caught in a sandstorm, place a wet cloth over your nose and mouth to help you breathe. Wear long trousers, or your legs will be blasted by grains of sand.

These rock formations are in Monument Valley in Arizona, USA.

THE DEADLIEST DESERT

ANTARCTICA

• Dry Valleys

If you crossed the deadliest desert in the world you wouldn't have to worry about the heat! Antarctica has just 10 centimetres of snow each year, making Antarctica a desert. Antarctica is so dry that some parts are completely free of ice.

As well as being the coldest desert on Earth, **Antarctica** is also the windiest, highest, most isolated and least explored continent. If you want to explore an extreme habitat, look no further!

The **Dry Valleys** of Antarctica get almost no snowfall or moisture – they are even drier than the Sahara. The mountains blocked **glaciers** from moving into the valleys, leaving large areas of bare rock. Today, any moisture is soon sucked away by winds swooping down the valleys.

The Dry Valleys in Antarctica cover about 4,800 square kilometres.

DESERT SURVIVAL TIPS

The camels of the Gobi Desert can walk 50 km a day while carrying 140 kg of cargo. Even today, camels move almost 30 per cent of the cargo that passes across the Gobi Desert.

Wild camels in the cold Gobi Desert survive by eating snow rather than drinking water.

DESERT NOTEBOOK

- Some places in Antarctica haven't had any rain for four million years!

- In winter, temperatures in the Antarctic can fall to −88°C, making it the coldest place on Earth.

Snow leopard

- The mountains of the Gobi Desert are home to the beautiful snow leopard, which hunts wild sheep, mountain goats and rabbits. Few people have ever seen this shy creature in the wild.

- There are cold deserts in many parts of the world. The Great Basin Desert in the western USA is a cold desert.

The Gobi Desert is another cold desert. In winter, temperatures fall to -40°C. In northwest China, a region of the Gobi Desert is called the Takla Makan Desert. Its name means "Go in and you won't come out again!"

DESERT WONDERS

Even if you survive the heat, dust and wind of the desert, you might not get over its beauty! You can climb tall pillars of rock, explore deep canyons and walk across sand dunes shaped like crescents or stars.

Minerals in the rock give the Vermillion Cliffs in Utah, USA their red colour.

Uluru, in the central desert of Australia, is the largest single rock in the world. It is about 2 kilometres long and 2.5 kilometres wide.

DESERT SURVIVAL TIPS
Avoid walking across a desert during the hottest hours of the day. Plane-crash survivors have walked over 550 kilometres in 20 days by walking only at night.

At different times of the day, the rock appears to change colour from blue to violet to glowing red. It is sacred to the local Anangu people and ancient paintings decorate its cave walls.

Uluru in Australia is made from a type of sandstone that makes it appear to glow at sunrise and sunset.

El Tatio geysers in the Atacama Desert, in Chile.

DESERT NOTEBOOK

- Every year drivers race through the Sahara Desert during the Paris to Dakar rally. In 1983, 40 drivers had to be rescued after losing their way in a sandstorm.

A camel race in the Arabian Desert.

Visit the Painted Desert in Arizona, USA at sunrise or sunset. The rocks and sand will shine in a rainbow of colours, from purple to yellow, brown and red.

Deserts are full of surprises. 4,300 metres up, in the Atacama Desert in Chile, are the amazing El Tatio **geysers**. These shoot pillars of water and steam up to five metres into the air. In the nearby hills is the 150 metre deep Chiu-Chiu Lagoon, a lake right in the middle of the desert.

- Camels are also raced over the desert. Their top speed is over 30 kilometres per hour.

FACTFILE:

Plant Survivors

Only the toughest plants can live in a desert. Many are built to collect and store water. As a result, desert plants look unlike plants living in other habitats.

Desert locust

- Plants that store water often grow sharp spines to stop desert animals eating them.

- When there is a rain storm, seeds sprout, grow and bloom in just a few weeks. They can turn even a dry desert into a carpet of colourful flowers.

- When rain occurs in some dry areas of Africa and Asia, it can trigger a giant swarm of desert locusts.

- The swarm contains billions of locusts, and they eat everything in their path. Locust swarms can lead to **famine** for local people.

HOW DO CACTI SURVIVE IN THE DESERT?

Instead of leaves, cacti have sharp spines that stop animals from eating them.

Cacti grow slowly, but some can live for 200 years.

Folded shape to allow cactus to swell up with water when it rains.

Their tough, waxy skin seals in the moisture.

Cacti can survive years of **drought** on water collected from a single rainfall.

Tough Plants

- ## Welwitschia plant
  - This plant has leaves which grow up to 4 metres long. They collect water from night-time sea-fog and send it to the plant's roots.
  - It lives in the Namib Desert in Africa.
  - Some plants may live for as long as 2,000 years.

Welwitschia plant

- ## Baobab tree
  - The tree has no leaves for most of the year.
  - The leaves sprout only during the short rainy season.
  - Its large trunk stores water for the nine dry months ahead. It is native to Africa and Australia.

Baobab tree

- ## Jumping cholla
  - This cactus has stems that fall off so easily they seem to jump out and bite you when you pass by.
  - This helps the cholla spread to new areas.
  - The roots of a 1 metre tall cholla cover an area the size of a tennis court.

Jumping cholla

The Desert Paintbrush survives in the dry desert by taking water from the roots of neighbouring plants.

FACTFILE:

Animal Survivors

Desert animals need special bodies to cope with the dryness, the baking heat during the day and the bitter cold at night.

The red kangaroo from Australia can go for months without drinking at all.

- Smaller animals survive by avoiding heat. The tiny elf owl shelters from the hot desert sunlight inside a saguaro cactus.

- Larger animals survive by moving around, and will travel a long way from one **water hole** to the next.

- Many desert animals have pale coloured skin, feathers or fur. This keeps them cool by reflecting sunlight. Light colours reflect the sun better than dark colours.

How are people and camels adapted to survive in the desert?

	PERSON	CAMEL
DAYS WITHOUT WATER	1 day	20 days
AMOUNT DRUNK IN 10 MINUTES	2 litres	100 litres
EYELASHES (TO PREVENT SAND IN EYES)	1 set	3 sets
ABILITY TO WALK ON SAND	Bad – feet sink in sand.	Good – has tough soles and spreads its weight on four broad feet.
OTHER ADAPTATIONS	The ability to use tools and fire, and work in groups means that people can live comfortably in the desert.	Camels have a hump that stores fat for times when food is scarce. They also have a light coloured coat to reflect the Sun and a tough mouth to eat spiny desert plants.

Tricks for Survival

- **Jerboa**
  - Its long legs help it to move quickly over the hot desert sand.
  - It gets its water from seeds, and so it does not need to drink.
  - It does not sweat and it has very dry droppings.

Jerboa

- **Honeypot ants**
  - Honeypot ants gather nectar from flowers during the rainy season and feed it to special worker ants.
  - These workers store the nectar in their bodies. During the dry summer season they spit out the nectar for the rest of the colony to feed on.

Honeypot ant

- **Sandgrouse**
  - A male sandgrouse will fly up to 160 kilometres a day to find water.
  - It soaks up the water with its belly feathers. Then it flies home, bringing the water to its thirsty chicks.

Sandgrouse

- Pale colours are also a good form of camouflage, helping the animals to blend in with the sand or rocks.

- Some animals avoid the hot Sun by going underground. The American spadefoot toad spends most of the year in a deep underground burrow. It only comes out to lay its eggs during the rainy season.

Spadefoot toad

FACTFILE:

Desert Hunters

The gila monster is the largest North American lizard.

Even big hunters such as lions can survive in a desert. They get water from the blood of their prey. Many predators living in the desert hunt at night, keeping cool in rocky dens or burrows during the day.

- Some desert animals, like kingsnakes and geckos, have large eyes perfect for hunting at night.

- Other animals such as scorpions, use their senses of touch and smell to hunt in the dark.

DESERT FOOD WEB

This diagram is a simple food web. It shows how desert predators rely on other animals for food. The red arrows point from the food to the animal that eats it.

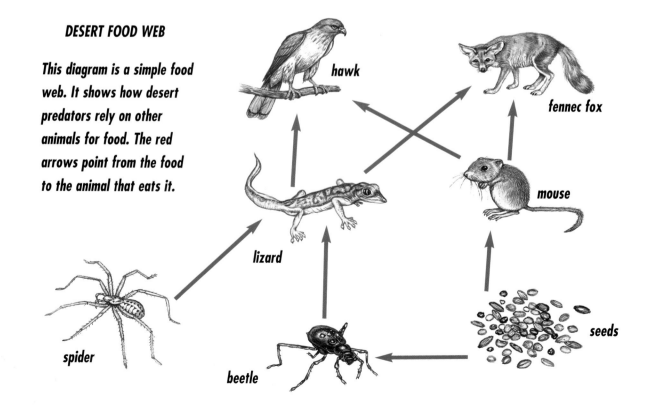

hawk

fennec fox

mouse

lizard

spider

seeds

beetle

Desert Hunters

- ## Vulture
  - Vultures escape the midday heat by soaring high into the cool air.
  - They also cool their legs by peeing on them!

Vulture

- ## Sidewinder snake
  - This snake moves over the hot sand in a special way, so that only a small part of its body touches the hot sand at any time.
  - It hunts by burying itself in sand and waiting for prey.

Sidewinder

- ## Roadrunner
  - A roadrunner can run at 27 kilometres per hour.
  - This is quick enough to catch a rattlesnake. The roadrunner snaps up the snake by the tail and slams its head against the ground until it is dead.

- ## Fennec fox
  - A fennec fox's large ears help it listen out for prey when hunting at night.
  - During the day, air passes over the fox's ears, which helps it to cool off.

Roadrunner

- Many desert creatures such as snakes, scorpions and spiders have venomous bites or stings. Food is difficult to find in a desert, and venom stops their victims from running away!

A rattlesnake may rattle its tail to warn potential predators that it is venomous.

FACTFILE:

Desert People

Surviving in the desert depends on finding food and water. In the past, desert people stayed alive by moving from place to place. They camped wherever they stopped.

A yurt is a tent used by the Mongols of the Gobi Desert. The yurt can be easily moved, which is necessary for a nomadic people.

- Some desert people, such as the Bedouins and the Tuareg, are **herders** and **traders**.

- Camels, goats and sheep give **nomadic** people meat, milk, wool and skins.

- The San people are **hunters**. They live in family groups and hunt small mammals.

- The Native Australians are also hunters. They look for food such as wallabies, witchetty grubs, insects and berries.

Witchetty grubs are sometimes eaten raw!

Wallabies are found throughout Australia.

This chart lists some groups of people who live in the world's major deserts.

DESERT	PEOPLE
ARABIAN	BEDOUINS
AUSTRALIA	NATIVE AUSTRALIANS
GOBI	MONGOLS
KALAHARI	SAN
SAHARA	TUAREG

Bedouin Survival Techniques

- ## Headcloth
  - This is wrapped around the head and often covers the neck as well.
  - The headcloth is a shield from the Sun and provides protection against the cold.
  - One end can be brought up to cover the nose and mouth, to keep the wind and sand out.

- ## Tracking
  - Tracking is a traditional skill, and was used to help the Bedouin hunt wild animals.
  - A Bedouin may be able to spot the footprint of a relative as easily as you would recognise a friend's photo.

- ## Collecting water
  - One Bedouin trick is to turn over half-buried stones in the desert just before the Sun rises. Fine drops of water form on the stones' cool surface.

Bedouin headcloth

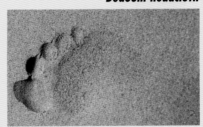

Footprint

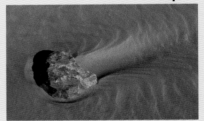

Stone in the desert

A Native Australian woman digs for grubs, which are a good source of protein.

FACTFILE:

Desert Threat

Windmills like this are sometimes used to pump water in desert areas.

The lack of water makes deserts unsuitable land for farming. Other land is also becoming unsuitable, mostly due to poor farming techniques. This increase in unuseable land is known as desertification.

- The areas around deserts are at risk of **desertification**. People must use the land carefully in order to farm there. Unfortunately, the people living near deserts are often poor, and they cut down trees for firewood. Without trees, there is little to stop the unproductive land from spreading.

People herd animals on the edges of the desert.

Soon, nothing can grow at all. The desert has spread.

Why are deserts spreading?

The animals eat the plants and the soil becomes thin and dry.

Without plant roots to hold it in place, the soil blows away.

Plant roots hold soil in place.

Desert Problems

- ● **Groundwater**
  - Many people live in cities in desert areas, such as Las Vegas in the USA.
  - Modern cities need lots of water.
  - Machines pump water from deep underground up to the desert surface.
  - This water may be used up faster than it can be replaced.

- ● **Roads**
  - Cities and busy roads make life difficult for big animals such as mountain lions.
  - They need large wild areas to roam in, away from cars and humans.

- ● **Mining**
  - There are many riches in the desert, such as oil, minerals, gold and diamonds.
  - Mining creates a lot of pollution.
  - It also causes **soil erosion**, leading to desertification.

Las Vegas

Mountain lion

Mining

This map shows the areas around the Sahara Desert which are at risk of becoming deserts.

Sahara Desert

KEY

 Desert

 Severe risk

Moderate risk

- ● There are some positive developments that will slow the spread of deserts. Trees and tough grasses are being planted on the edges of deserts to stop them from spreading.

- ● In some areas, **canals** transfer water from lakes and rivers into desert areas.

GLOSSARY

algae – simple plants which live in water, many of which can only be seen with a microscope.

Atacama Desert – a very dry desert in Chile, South America. It is long and narrow, about 150 kilometres wide and 1,000 kilometres long.

canals – waterways that are built to carry boats, or to take water from one place to another.

Death Valley – a very dry area in California in the United States, receiving less than 5 centimetres of rain a year. It is the site of the highest recorded temperature in the United States (56.7°C in 1913).

desertification – the way unproductive land is spreading because of human behaviour.

drought – a long period of very little rain.

Dry Valleys – the area in Antarctica that is not covered with ice and snow.

Equator – the imaginary line drawn around the middle of the Earth. It divides the world into a southern half and a northern half.

erg – a large area of sand dunes.

famine – an extreme shortage of food.

fulgurite – glass-like shapes formed when lightning strikes sand.

geyser – a hot spring which shoots water and steam into the air.

glaciers – large masses of ice.

global warming – the gradual increase in the world's temperature.

Gobi Desert – a large cold desert covering parts of China and Mongolia, in Asia. Winter temperatures average -40°C, while summer temperatures can reach 45°C.

herders – a group of people who keep herds of sheep, goats, horses or camels.